GW00375017

PAGE LEFT INTENTIONALLY BLANK

Page Left Intentionally Blank

Please see the whole collection on Amazon at:

PAGE LEFT INTENTIONALLY BLANK

PLEASE SEE THE WHOLE COLLECTION ON AMAZON AT:

Page Left Intentionally Blank

Please see the whole collection on Amazon at:

https://www.amazon.com/stores/author/b0bwsq1k7l/allbooks

Page Left Intentionally Blank

All contents of this publication are
Copyright Mark Cole 2023

Please see the whole collection on
Amazon at:

Page Left Intentionally Blank

All contents of this publication are
Copyright Mark Cole 2023

Page Left Intentionally Blank

All contents of this publication are
Copyright Mark Cole 2023

Please see the whole collection on
Amazon at:

Page Left Intentionally Blank

All contents of this publication are
Copyright Mark Cole 2023

Please see the whole collection on
Amazon at:

PAGE LEFT INTENTIONALLY BLANK

PLEASE SEE THE WHOLE COLLECTION ON
AMAZON AT:

Page Left Intentionally Blank

All contents of this publication are
Copyright Mark Cole 2023

Please see the whole collection on
Amazon at:

PAGE LEFT INTENTIONALLY BLANK

ALL CONTENTS OF THIS PUBLICATION ARE
COPYRIGHT MARK COLE 2023

PLEASE SEE THE WHOLE COLLECTION ON
AMAZON AT:

PAGE LEFT INTENTIONALLY BLANK

Page Left Intentionally Blank

All contents of this publication are
Copyright Mark Cole 2023

Please see the whole collection on
Amazon at:

Page Left Intentionally Blank

All contents of this publication are
Copyright Mark Cole 2023

Please see the whole collection on
Amazon at:

Page Left Intentionally Blank

All contents of this publication are Copyright Mark Cole 2023

Please see the whole collection on Amazon at:

PAGE LEFT INTENTIONALLY BLANK

PLEASE SEE THE WHOLE COLLECTION ON
AMAZON AT:

Page Left Intentionally Blank

Please see the whole collection on
Amazon at:

PAGE LEFT INTENTIONALLY BLANK

ALL CONTENTS OF THIS PUBLICATION ARE
COPYRIGHT MARK COLE 2023

PLEASE SEE THE WHOLE COLLECTION ON
AMAZON AT:

PAGE LEFT INTENTIONALLY BLANK

ALL CONTENTS OF THIS PUBLICATION ARE
COPYRIGHT MARK COLE 2023

PLEASE SEE THE WHOLE COLLECTION ON
AMAZON AT:

PAGE LEFT INTENTIONALLY BLANK

ALL CONTENTS OF THIS PUBLICATION ARE
COPYRIGHT MARK COLE 2023

PLEASE SEE THE WHOLE COLLECTION ON
AMAZON AT:

Page Left Intentionally Blank

All contents of this publication are
Copyright Mark Cole 2023

Please see the whole collection on
Amazon at:

Page Left Intentionally Blank

All contents of this publication are
Copyright Mark Cole 2023

Please see the whole collection on
Amazon at:

Page Left Intentionally Blank

All contents of this publication are
Copyright Mark Cole 2023

Please see the whole collection on
Amazon at:

Page Left Intentionally Blank

Printed in Great Britain
by Amazon

33202849R00044